A Busy Day at Mr. Kang's Grocery Store

Written by
ALICE K. FLANAGAN

Photographs by
CHRISTINE OSINSKI

Reading Consultant
LINDA CORNWELL
Learning Resource Consultant
Indiana Department Of Education

CHILDREN'S PRESS® *A Division of Grolier Publishing*
New York • London • Hong Kong • Sydney • Danbury, Connecticut

Special thanks to Seuk-Ho Kang for allowing us to tell his story.

Also, thanks to Jung Hwa Shin for her assistance.

Library of Congress Cataloging-in-Publication Data
Flanagan, Alice.
    A busy day at Mr. Kang's grocery store / by Alice K. Flanagan; photographs by Christine Osinski; reading consultant, Linda Cornwell.
        p. cm. — (Our neighborhood)
    Summary: Describes the work done each day by a Korean American who owns the neighborhood grocery store.
    ISBN 0-516-20047-X (lib. bdg.)—0-516-26061-8 (pbk.)
    1. Grocers—United States—Juvenile literature. 2. Korean Americans—Juvenile literature. 3. Grocery trade—Management—Juvenile literature.
[1. Grocery trade. 2. Occupations.] I. Osinski, Christine, ill. II. Title.
III. Series: Our neighborhood (New York, N.Y.)
    HD8039.G82U63   1996
    381'.148'0973—dc20   96-17144
                                                                         CIP
                                                                          AC

Photographs ©: Christine Osinski

Meet my neighbor, Mr. Kang.
He owns this grocery store.

Every morning,
at eight o'clock sharp,
he looks out the window
and unlocks the front door.

Mr. Kang has a lot to do
before the customers come—

sweep the floor,

arrange the fruit,

and put out fresh flowers.

Mr. Kang must fill
the cash register drawer

and order supplies.

More fresh fruit has been delivered.

There are cartons of milk
to count and unpack.

Mr. Kang welcomes the customers,
and fills all their needs.

Fresh fruit?

A bouquet of flowers?

Some vegetables, please!

Mrs. Kang also works in the store.

Together, Mr. and Mrs. Kang help their customers.

18

Mr. and Mrs. Kang have two children.

The Kang family lives upstairs, above the small store.

Six years ago, they left Korea
and came to America to start
their own business.

It wasn't easy
learning new things—

a new language, new customs,
new schools for the children.

But, Mr. Kang worked hard and made his dream come true.

He is generous and kind
and has made many new friends.

Now everyone in our neighborhood
goes to Mr. Kang's store

to buy fresh fruit, flowers, or a cup
of hot tea.

Every evening at nine o'clock
when Mr. Kang locks the front door,
he is tired, but happy, to go home
to his family.

Meet the Author
and the Photographer

Alice Flanagan and Christine Osinski are sisters. They grew up together telling stories and drawing pictures in a brown brick bungalow in a southwest-side neighborhood of Chicago, Illinois. Today they write stories and take photographs professionally.

Ms. Flanagan resides in Chicago with her husband and works as a freelance writer. Ms. Osinski is a photographer and teaches at The Cooper Union for the Advancement of Science and Art in New York City. She lives with her husband and two sons on Staten Island.